Poems of Recovered Joy

by

N.M. Rai

Rai, N.M.

Poems of Recovered Joy

ISBN: 978-1-4357-2802-8

Published by Lulu

Cover Design by N.M. Rai

Dedication:

This book is dedicated to everyone
who has walked the path from pain
to joy in “a company of goodly friends”.

The Serenity Prayer

God grant us the serenity to accept the
things we cannot change, the courage
to change the things we can, and
the wisdom to know the difference.

Table of Contents

--

hungers

we sit in a circle
of goodly friends
speaking of stars
and morning light

and how our bones
ached from emptiness
when we wandered lost
in night hungers

watching

I drifted out to sea
on a raft with no oars
till saw myself
standing on the shore
speaking into the wind
the way seagulls do
and I was too far away
to hear the emptiness.

paws

we meet daily now
and have learned
like dragons do
how to sidestep
each other's spines
how to sit in a circle
and shake paws
without the need to roar

houses

even now
I love cloud walking

that feel
of wild wings
on my back
and sun whispers

I know moments
like this
but no longer build
houses there

whatever it is

we want it now
whatever it is

we need to fill
the hole in us
that itches
that runs across
our minds
till we forget
names and voices

as we stumble
in the moment
stuffing ourselves
with illusion

threads

you speak and
we switch clothes
my fears
drip on your skin

we see our eyes
in another's face
and climb
hand over hand
across the threads
that bind us

ice

I walk into my head
and find ice fields
landscapes
frozen and empty
without markers
or roads

I chew moonlight
and grasp at sounds
waiting for ghosts
to appear
you arrive
and the ice melts

full

we eat time
slowly

moons wither
and snow falls
yet still we sit
always in the now
then it is years
and we are full

we toss our lives
like crumbs on the trail
for those walking
in our footsteps

joy

joy arrived
in tattered clothes
peeked in the door

we told it to go away
we were afraid
of strangers
whose language
we didn’t know

years

I spent years
speaking in the wind
frostbitten in dreams

no one answered

now I live in a garden and
music falls from my lips

dragons

I blow them out of glass
transparent suns
rising like sunflowers
in soul fields
armies of them
fall from my breath
till I have no place
left to walk
in the glittering fears
of my imagining

wings

we can't live
as amputees
as caterpillars
without feet
sliced in half
and yearning

we grow wings
and don't miss walking

lips

I spoke a strange language
as if I didn't know verbs
stepped on stones of difference
though I never asked
if anyone else felt this way
this not fitting
like the child who cried
the emperor has no clothes
and went home lashed by lips
that sneered "how could you"

Icarus

it's that leap into the sun
that seduced
as if we had burst
and become the universe
Icarus
with unmelted wings

flows

I flew in my own mind
in the heat
of an inner volcano
in flows of pleasure
neuron fired dreams
that existed nowhere

too loud

the silence
is too loud
sitting becalmed
in a rowboat
surrounded by
sleeping gulls
in horizon-less
moments

boxes

we consumed
with greedy hands
and puckered lips

there was never enough
of this liquid gold
with the taste of desire

that left us
skin-wrapped
with torn edges
leaking light
into dark boxes
with stone lids

gifts

we often
strangle moments
with thoughts
run wild

spinning images
of a future
that always
drowns dark

while our nows
are gifts
of pure water
left untasted

eyes

you come new
into our world

we give you
our eyes
and you weep
with relief

scars

your pain
bleeds onto me
and I taste
my healed scars
that tell me you're kin

ravens

I once cowered
under squawking ravens
who lived inside me
dark and invisible as fear

euphoria

they called it euphoria
that flood of joy
that numbed the senses
till we became the light
in our own minds
and spoke with a voice
we didn't realize
was not our own

tigers

you tell me of the tigers
in your morning coffee
how their roars
dislocated your ears
how your parachute
didn't open last night and
you woke up with scolding
voices in your head

I show you pictures
of my own tigers
before they left and
coffee became just coffee

cemeteries

we have cemeteries
in our heads
of undead thoughts
and exhausted desires

sometimes they rise up
put on clothes
and strut into the morning
speaking of the old fires
the treks up mountains

we do not shake hands

edges

it's easier to draw
pain than joy
pain has
sharper edges
and joy disappears
into everything

blank walls

the taste of oranges
is fleeting
you have to pay attention
to see rainbows

it's too easy
to look through lazy lids
at blank walls
and wonder where life is

dogs

the dogs protected me
in the worst of it
I slept with them
when the walls wept
they chewed my fear
like bones
in front of my eyes

taste

the sun
melts my hands
tulips wear
the plumage of birds

I live in
moments
with the taste
of eternity

day one

we were all
the uncrowned kings
of our own worlds
dispossessed
into a sobriety
we had yet to understand

I am

I am a location
in space
a pinch of dough
from the eternal bread
a single breath
of the divine
I am one hand
reaching

never

we are never alone now
crouched in corners
in our minds
weeping moments
as if
they were tears

rip currents

fears drift like sand
on bare feet
rip currents from the past
that grab unexpectedly
you taught me to swim
parallel to the shore.

tolls

there's a cost
I keep paying tolls
it's painless
this constant attention
which becomes
a pleasure
as my life expands
and you sew wings
on my shoulders
and I learn to sing

legion

my family is legion
I who was so alone
an alien life form
in my own mind
who startled small dogs
on city streets
can now fly to anywhere
and know I am home

veils

we fell off the beanstalk
halfway to the cloud
the reality of things
escaped us
as we danced
in our minds
stitched to the veils
of our own perceptions

mice

we had demands
of what was supposed to be
jigsaw puzzles we wove
in our child minds
with magic words
for the monsters under the bed

if we could just get it right
rearrange the pieces
find the formula
in the mess of our days
but we were locked out
failures again
chasing hours
like demented mice

sunflowers

I never knew
I had an iron cage
around my lungs
till you unlocked it
and I walked free
in meadows
with sunflowers
taller than myself

parents

our parents
were always mysteries
like Easter Island statues
come to life
they did not speak
of themselves
we are left to imagine
the intricacies of tall clouds

brooms

you are hesitant
like the first drops of rain
you smile at the air
as if it would bite
like nightmares
spilled into the day
we grab brooms
and they flee

open

you drop in
you're in town
our door is open
you speak
of my childhood
though we've never met

we run there
together
into the tree-house
of forgotten dreams

variations

I am often lost
in night dreams
running down stairs
for 15 floors
to find only
locked doors or

stumbling at night
on tilted streets
I don't recognize
variations on a theme
of years
that weren't dreams

upside down

we gather like magpies
on rooftops
speak of where the hawks
are hunting today
which bird feeders are full
how the cat got teased

of the ordinary things
we never noticed
when we flew upside down
with wings on fire

fears

fears fit like too tight clothes
that constrict the day
and are difficult to name
as they have no faces

beginnings

we're stranded in the airport
eating stale crackers at 3 am
talking to ourselves
in restroom mirrors
stumbling on the words of
this new language
dancing to a beat
we'd never imagined

weeds

I've been eating weeds
salting them with
fears and questions
till they ferment
in my mind and
sour the day

home

we crack pinatas
and red feathered parrots
fly out screeching joy
asking where we've been

returned

we have debts
we can never repay
when your hands
pulled me from the mud
wiped my eyes
and breathed on me
I returned
like Lazarus

we were

we were naked birds
imagining feathers
leaping off rooftops
expecting to fly

lions

I'm a terrible archer
always missing the mark
overshooting into trees
breaking shafts against rocks
dropping arrows from the bow
losing track of things
so I walk around wearing this cap
that says hopeless at archery
lions can't fish and
antelope don't climb trees

as if I know

I pour the day
into my bowl
along with the cereal
without thought
as if I know
its contents
and which spoon
to use

rumbles

we hold you
in these crises
that shake
the day
and send
the mind reeling
then turn
and fall into you
when our own earth
rumbles

it was

it was the feel
of being a bark beetle
swigging the sap
of dying trees
hiding from light
that stumble
into open spaces
where the beaks
of crows waited
for undefined moments
and unwary bodies
and mornings arrived
like stillborn eggs

afterthought

fears arise
almost without notice
like the first drops
of a flood
a mere scent
moistening air
a tightening of muscles
below conscious mind
in this flesh we live in
like an afterthought
the way a page is
to a word

now

hope has stained my skin
and I live now
painted in joy

ourselves

we forgive ourselves
for not being our dreams
for having no wings
for our feet that stumble
and how easily
we erased ourselves
trying to hide our fears

unborn

you moved into my mind
and parts of me
that were unborn
opened their eyes

no need

these are moments when
we butter contentment
on our skin and smiles
grow tall as daisies

there is no need to speak
of how we warm each other

riverbeds

we are everywhere
like muddied stones
in riverbeds
aching for sunlight

hitting bottom

we didn’t know
we’d sculpted our world
stepped off cliffs
and raised our swords
to battle the dragons
in our minds

till doom settled in
like dust and
nothing breathed
as we listened
for stilled voices
in emptied rooms

nestlings

we are nestlings
amazed at our wings
hopping on one foot
daring to taste joy

skulls

when we wake in ice fields
drinking from skulls
with the world torn
behind our eyes

we remember this will pass
like clouds above a river

you told me

you told me
I had a problem

now I'd found
the answer
and all I had to do
was let it happen
and I did
and it did

ease

we have the ease of family
that knowing under the skin
the acceptance of oddities
like the uncle who knew
tomatoes were poison
so we never put any
on his plate

bottom of the glass

we ate ourselves
in our hunger
grabbed at years
in the moment
saw passing clouds
as the ocean

fell through
the bottom of the glass
into inner caves
where ravenous
demons deafened us
with their roars

forgotton

I didn’t know I’d forgotten
the sound of birdsong
till I woke one morning
wondering what I heard

skitter

sometimes
you are just tired
or feeling lonely
and memories
skitter like ants
over sugar

fear

fear can twist you
like heavy laundry
till your eyes
are caught in the folds
and you're left blind
clawing the dampness

whispers

you tell me your story

your feelings are
so like my own
as if we came from
the same egg
or the same dream

possibilities

we walk
into possibilities
even in the darkness
of blind tunnels

on demand

we bought bliss on demand
that left us skinned and bleeding
on leftover mornings
trying to bargain with God

surrender

we celebrate
the anniversaries
of our surrender
to what was

and is
and would become

when hopelessness
hid behind doors
of fear
without horizons

if

if you were not here
I should fall
stuttering raw sounds
wordless

thrown back
like a too small fish
into the sea of myself
deaf to the light

just met

we’ve just met
yet we both know
those night corridors
where we ate terrors
while hunting
for the taste of joy

anchor

we anchor each other
we who used to stumble
through clouds
thirsting after raindrops

and tumble down
the beanstalks of fairy tales

always upended
and contrary

thorns

you can be difficult
as can I

we no longer throw
boiling oil
over the battlements
or chase after dragons

our armor is
stowed away and rusting
yet we still have thorns
that can prick the unwary

ten years

it’s been ten years
since you fell
into these rooms
and I saw you move
like a glittering ghost
among the tables

when

when my tongue
follows my mind
and the day tastes
like metal
we speak
and you say
“I know”

swallow

we were rolling hungers
trying to swallow
the world

fly

a part of us still
secretly believes
we can fly

we no longer walk backwards
with our eyes closed

waters

once again I stepped
onto seaweed
as if I could walk
into the next moment
on waters of wanting
strong enough to hold me

often

we speak often
during the week
like birds on a wire
checking in

leaning

we laugh
at the old disasters

we share the joys
which leave us
leaning like trees
in winds of amazement

glimpses

life is richer today
less crazy

but there are glimpses
now and then
of fires seen
through pinholes in the sky

and we remember the taste
of the flames

bubble

I walked around
inside a bubble
talking to myself
and never saw
the nails
on the sidewalk

stirred

always that restlessness
as if we were being stirred
or there were bees
under the skin

we shivered like wet dogs
but it clung to us

the only answer we knew
was one more

eagerly

we wait eagerly for a meeting
on those afternoons
when we've erased ourselves
in our own minds

sailed

we understand the stories
of each other's lives

we know where
the flowers bloom

back

looking back
we'd buttered ourselves
with impossible dreams
and slid off our lives
in tangles of grasping

www.ingramcontent.com/pod-product-compliance
Ingram Content Group UK Ltd.
Pitfield, Milton Keynes, MK11 3LW, UK
UKHW041928190726
13854UKWH00004B/1501